The Camouflaged Sacred

A Collection of Poetry, Liturgy & Prayer

By Joanna Hargreaves

To my children,
who are walking poetry
and answered prayers.

Copyright © 2021 by Joanna Hargreaves
ISBN: 9798483707844
All rights reserved.

No part of this book may be reproduced or used in any manner without written permission of the copyright owner except for the use of quotations in a book review.

For more information contact:
camouflagedsacred@gmail.com

Edited by Meghan Bell
Design by Joseph Bell

Praise for *The Camouflaged Sacred*

The Camouflaged Sacred is a masterpiece! It has taken my breath away, healed me, revived me, challenged me and comforted me all at the same time. The combination of the mundane and divine woven together is so beautiful. These poems soothe, uplift, encourage and will make you smile. The prayers are an anchor, life-raft and spiritual "first aid kit" if you find your own words and needs can't be expressed amongst the busyness of life. Thank you Jo for this book - it's pure treasure and a healing balm.

Sally Beaton, author of *Get Your Sparkle Back*, **founder of** *Women With Sparkle*

I have always enjoyed looking into the meaning and richness of words. The Bible says they are powerful, both negatively and positively. In this first book, *The Camouflaged Sacred*, Jo wisely handles words in a way that makes the greater qualities of life accessible. Though not afraid to challenge or surprise, she crafts sentences in such a way that negative emotions are disarmed and the honourable things of life are unearthed. This book has the potential to push back clouds on a rainy day, allowing light to shine through. A great resource for thinking, imagining, reflecting and stimulating prayer.

Stuart Bell, Senior Pastor of *Alive Church*, **author of** *Mud In The Eye, Sane Spirituality, Rebuilding the Walls* **and** *The Name*

Jo Hargreaves' words provide a balm for the hurting, a sword for the fighting and steadiness for the searching as she speaks of the love found in the Divine. Jo advocates for others to experience freedom and joy, using words of truth to dismantle the enemy of the human heart who schemes to deflate hope. *The Camouflaged Sacred* is a gift to all who read it. Jo embodies this work. Her life is a testimony, and her words inspire us to follow suit.

Connie Armerding - Executive Coach / Leadership Consultant at LIVINGWHOLEHEARTED LLC.

In *The Camouflaged Sacred*, Jo explores themes of sanctification & vocation with empathy honesty & humanity

She invites us to look beneath the surface of things, beyond what they appear to be, beyond our assumptions into a careful & playful examination of God at work - unhurried and constant in our daily patterns of life.

This book serves as an invitation to recognise a God we have overlooked, to acknowledge His being at the intersection of our humanity & His divinity. Jo gives us language that invite the making and remaking of His Holy Spirit, that disarms the stormtroopers of religion & points us down the path of a constant communion in the swirl & humdrum of modern life.

If you are dissatisfied with a micro managed religious performance and ache to experience the fullness of all that God has for you, then Jo's words will help you get there"

Matt and Claire Hooper, founders of Kingdom Company

As I was reading *The Camouflaged Sacred*, I lost count of the moments I was shocked by how accurately someone else could express emotions and thoughts I so often experience. Jo's power of relatability really shines in this volume. She creates a space where you are welcomed to commune with Jesus, hear the Father's voice and receive the breath and life of the Holy Spirit wherever you are in your day to day life, whether that's folding laundry or pondering the complexity of existence, or both at once!

I think this work is inspired, and a timely tool to help us to connect with Jesus in a deep and beautiful way. May you receive His love as you linger in these pages. They are sure to break down walls and show you more of who He is, and who you are.

Meghan Bell, author of *Desired Child*, *The Glass Country* and *Anthology Volume I: Unearthing*

Contents

Foreword	i
Introduction	iii
Poetry	1
Prayer & Liturgy	57
Acknowledgements	94
About the Author	96

Foreword
by Leah Boden

In 2017, we moved house. I diligently de cluttered, donated and designed a system for the boxes labelled "Boden family archives" which contained children's handprint pictures, wedding photos and a variety of note books from the late 90's filled with poetry. As I tentatively revisited these handwritten insights into my past, I was comforted by the place of poetry in these impressionable years. The journals held pages of reflections from my teen 'tragedies', travel observations, and the very humble beginnings of my spiritual formation.

I met Jo at a leaders conference in Derbyshire when my children were young, and hers were even younger. Jo was juggling young motherhood, church leadership, along with all the passion and vision she still holds today. We caught each other's eye in the entrance to the main hall, and both drew on our extroverted introversion to begin a friendship based on "go deep or go home"! Jo is a woman of deep conviction, yet is openly on a journey of spiritual construction. Her publicly shared poetry, prose and liturgy has gently revealed to us elements of her 'travels'; *The Camouflaged Sacred* takes us further.

The poet Luci Shaw tells us that "Like all art, poems are only hints and guesses that draw our attention to something larger." *The Camouflaged Sacred* collection doesn't make assumptions of the reader, it doesn't hand us finished pieces of spiritual formula, or authoritatively tell us what to do. *The*

Camouflaged Sacred draws our attention to something larger and invites us into that same journey.

This collection isn't highfalutin lip service; *The Camouflaged Sacred* is for everyone, reminding us that "that miracles reside in the mundane, that the sacred, is often camouflaged."

Leah Boden
Leahboden.com
@leahvboden

Introduction

The poems and prayers contained within this book have been scribbled out in the snatched moments; the school run moments, mid-food-shop moments, football practice sideline moments, or those frequent youth theatre rehearsal moments. You could say there is nothing spiritual or sacred about how or where they are written, no beautifully curated, antique writing bureau, no ink blotted parchment or typewriter. They are simply scribbled out in the humdrum of everyday, ordinary life. Isn't it just like God to show up there, right in the midst of the ordinary? Isn't it just like God to position the sacred things here, there and everywhere, so that they seem almost camouflaged to those who don't have eyes to see? His miraculous presence resides in the mundane, so that even the day-to-day moments become spaces to know Him.

This book is an invitation to re-centre what may have felt scattered and to remind ourselves of a God who is not distant but is closer than our own breath. It is an invitation to be seen, known and loved, to relax our shoulders and to exhale that breath we may have been unknowingly holding.

This book is for you, for me and for anyone who longs to see God in the everyday moments of life, the pairing of socks, the washing of dishes and all the other things on our lists. It is for those of us that want to lift our eyes to heaven but often get distracted by scrolling and swiping and adding to cart.
It is for those of us who get caught up in comparison, who need to be reminded that we bear the fingerprints of our creator and are called to show up for our own lives. It is for

those of us who can get tripped up by a bad day, who need the benediction of 'me too' and who ultimately just need to sit for a while so that we can remember both who and whose we are again.

So as you are reading, please know that I have prayed for you, I have prayed that you hear the whisper of the Father's love over you and the roar of your own heart. I pray that you feel connected to Jesus, and complete in His love. I pray that this books serves you and meets you exactly where you are.

You are so very loved.

POETRY

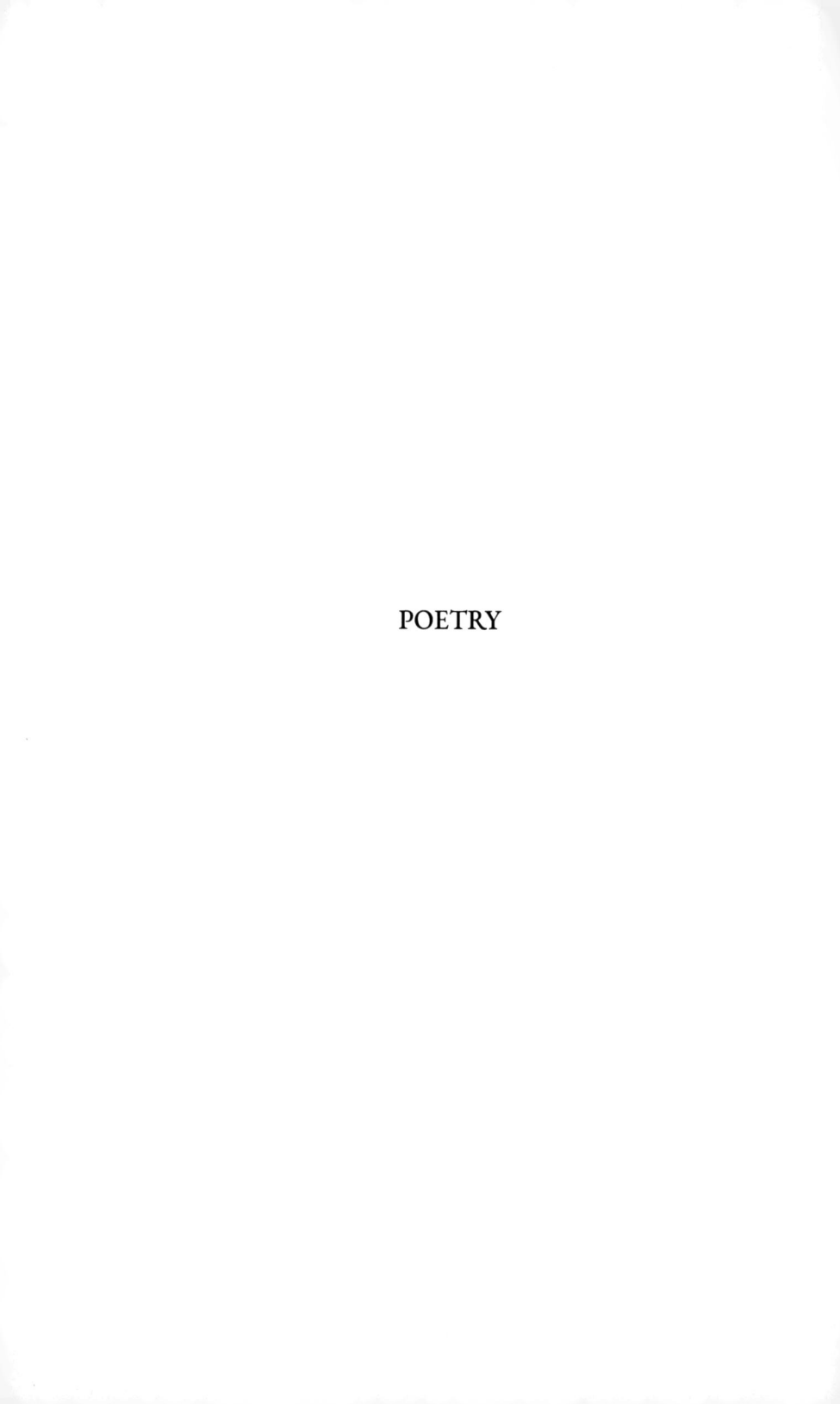

For When I Start To Feel Small

If I ever start to feel small,
tempted by the self protective lure
of shrinking and diminishing,
may I stand my sacred ground
even to the point of taking off my shoes,
because I am called to holy work on holy ground.
May I know the call,
to love and to be loved,
fully embodying the truth of my belovedness,
feet firmly planted,
spirit alive,
eyes wide open to the wonder of new possibilities
and the calling of fresh opportunities.

Our brokenness is never the starting point,

our belovedness is.

Blossom Tree

I have a blossom tree in my garden
and each day I watch and wait,
but the buds have not yet flowered
and yet, she's not a second late.
She's not concerned by those around her,
no need to force how she's designed,
she is contented in the waiting
and will blossom when it's her time.

Becoming Myself

Give me courage to grab with both hands,
the life-giving words
that speak of me as
being fearfully and wonderfully made.
May those same words pilgrimage
from my head to my heart,
from decorative fridge magnet theology,
to taking up space in my soul
and causing me
to become fully myself.

Socks

Amongst the hurry of the day
in the pairing of socks and the wiping of worktops,
may you find some time to get quiet
so that you can truly hear-
that God-given inner knowing
that stands up to all logic and reason,
and instead leads us into truth,
restoring our perspective
and setting us free.
Free indeed.

THE CAMOUFLAGED SACRED

Eyes To See

Today my worship will simply and profoundly be
to pay attention to all that is around me;
to lift my eyes, to open my heart,
and gently refuse to let it pass me by.
May I be receptive and soft-hearted enough
to be moved by the enormity of it all,
and to see that big answers can appear
in seemingly small ways.
Give me ears to hear and eyes to see
that miracles reside in the mundane,
that the sacred-
is often camouflaged.

**You are a story
that is still being written.**

Holy Adventure

May your faith
be less of an approval-based performance,
and more of a holy adventure.

Gratitude

*When I get that awkward feeling
that my life would just improve,
if I had bifold doors or tiled floors;
perhaps we should just move.
When I just can't shake that feeling
that my lot's not quite enough
and if I ran 10k to start my day
or had a wardrobe full of stuff,
if I labelled all my food jars
or signed up to HelloFresh,
I would feel just so much better
my life would not feel such a mess.
But when comparison starts to creep
into my heart and to my head,
I've learned it's time to just stop scrolling
and practice gratitude instead.*

A Tender Reminder

Today, for a little while
I felt heavy with a kind of sadness,
that weighed in my gut.
So I sat with it for a while
and allowed the overwhelming feeling
of scarcity to wash over me:
the things I never had,
the way I wish it had been,
the if onlys and the what ifs
that we accumulate
as life moves ever forward.
I did not need a cheering squad
or a steady hand to pull me up,
just a tender reminder
of the God who put on skin,
who neither slumbers nor sleeps.
Just a tender reminder that He sees.
He knows.
He loves.
Just a tender reminder.

Emmanuel

Emmanuel.
God with us,
with us then,
with us now;
willing to condescend and walk
in the dirt and mess
of our everyday humdrum human experience,
wearing His human skin;
not distant-
not distracted-
but with us.

**May my heart
host your presence.**

Permission

Today, I give myself permission
to fully show up.
I refuse to shrink
in order that others feel more comfortable.
I will not water myself down,
stroke egos or be dictated or distracted
by watching myself being watched.
I will instead
occupy the sacred space God has gifted me,
and I will fill it with my most true and authentic self.

Balm

The words 'me too'
are like a balm,
a benediction.
They wake me.
They shake me.
And they make me
brave.

I will no longer wage war with my inner critic. Instead, I will silence and soothe her with words of compassion.

Becoming

Help me to learn,
that the uncomfortable feeling
in which I feel like a fraud,
is just the small space,
between who I currently am-
and all I am becoming.

The Little Things

Sun on your face,
breath in your lungs,
the feeling of freshly washed hair,
a candle's crackle,
taking off your bra at the end of the day,
a book tentatively opened and the moment it connects,
a fresh piece of paper,
the first sip of hot tea,
opening the dishwasher to find it is empty,
a message from a friend,
a nostalgic song that reminds you of the girl you were,
a rush of creativity,
the cold side of the pillow,
a sense of holy presence,
a glimmer of hope.

Empty

If you ever feel empty,
may you remember deep in your bones
that an empty tomb was the stage
where a God-breathed plot twist
changed all of our narratives
for all of time.
Empty places and spaces,
empty tombs and wombs,
empty hands and plans,
even empty lunch boxes
are where God seems
to gloriously work out His ways.

Exhale

When my tension is high
and my tolerance low,
when I feel almost too unpalatable
to be considered holy,
would You remind me, Jesus,
that I'm welcome-
just as I am;
and that if I linger for a while,
my shoulders will relax
and I can exhale the breath,
I wasn't aware I had been holding.

Courage is contagious.
Courage is contagious.
Courage is contagious.
Courage is contagious.
Courage is contagious.
Courage is contagious.
Courage is contagious.
Courage is contagious.
Courage is contagious.
Courage is contagious.
Courage is contagious.
Courage is contagious.
Courage is contagious.
Courage is contagious.
Courage is contagious.
Courage is contagious.
Courage is contagious.
Courage is contagious.
Courage is contagious.
Courage is contagious.
Courage is contagious.
Courage is contagious.
Courage is contagious.
Courage is contagious.
Courage is contagious.
Courage is contagious.
Courage is contagious.
Courage is contagious.

Anchor

Oh, to you who is diminishing yourself
and keeping yourself small,
who gets caught in the waves
of questioning and second guessing;
to you who have gradually
distanced and danced yourself
away from you inner knowing,
so that now you feel all at sea:
may you remember as you feel adrift,
bobbing this way and that,
that you have an anchor,
a true north,
and that Jesus is your way home.

**A soft heart
is your superpower.**

Altar

Save me from worshiping
at the altar of myself and my own preference.
I remind my soul, all my wills,
my thoughts and my emotions,
that I am gloriously created in Your image-
not You in mine.
Help me to notice when I have strayed away
from deep, rich, transformative truth,
and have instead defaulted
to a pick and mix religion,
in which I never cease
to feel comfortable
and wholly justified in all my ways.

Untangled

I desire to be untangled from the places and spaces
in which I cannot show up as my full self;
where self-censorship keeps the peace
whilst robbing me of mine;
the rooms and tables
that cause me to forget that I am knitted
and instead leave me feeling knotted,
that cause me to feel confined and constricted,
obligated and restricted.
May I instead feel free, free indeed,
to show up,
as the truest version of myself.

Human

God, who is clothed in majesty,
yet who stepped into humanity,
who gently stooped and condescended
so you could look us eye to eye;
God, who wasn't too far removed
to feel a heart beating in your chest
and sweat on your brow,
who left majestic robes
to put on deep brown skin
that burned, and cracked, and shed,
would you show us better ways of being human,
of occupying our own skin and bones
in a way that embraces all that we are,
but that leaves room for all that we can be.

**Courage looks
so good on you.**

Good Friday

On that first Good Friday,
You picked up Your cross
and looked out across the whole of time,
past, present and future.
And there I stood.
The crowds gathered,
the jeering, the sneering,
contempt and rebellion thick in the air.
Your back lashed,
then spat at,
one nail, two nail, three nail, four.
There You hung,
arms outstretched,
an eternal invitation,
come one and come all.
As You tasted blood,
I tasted freedom.
As You poured out Your life,
mine began to make sense.
Your last breath given
in exchange that I can breathe You in
and breathe You out-
a holy symbiosis.

Father

If you have no frame of reference
for a Father who would take off his shoes
and run towards you,
who would throw a lavish party
to celebrate you even on your worst days,
or leave everything he was doing
in order to find you when you felt lost;
if that is not your experience,
then today may you get a glimpse
of the Father heart of God towards you
and may it feel like coming home.

Stay curious.

Sellotape

For the sellotape-end-finders
and the late-night-wrappers,
those who can't find their address book
or the big box of crackers,
those that are making lists and checking them twice
and who in the process feel not very nice,

for those who are planning and prepping and scheming,
letting go of the Christmas they might have been dreaming,
to those whose heads feel incredibly full
who are juggling the juggle
of work, home and school,

my prayer for you
is that you may find some space,
five minutes of peace where you step out of the race,
may you remember who you are and to whom you belong.
May you find some perspective
and recover your song.

And God bless to you
if you're doing that thing,
where you buy all the chocolate
then you buy it again
because around 10pm
when the scissors are lost
you seek out those chocolates
and eat the whole lot.

Twixt-mass

'Twas the bit after Christmas and all through the house,
no one can remember what day the bins should go out.
There's still enough Turkey to last until New Years Eve
and the fridge is now smelling quite strongly of Brie.

"Twas the bit after Christmas and under the tree
Is a pile of pine needles and a gift for Aunt Jean.
The Quality Street tin is depressingly bare
with only the coconut and orange ones there.

'Twas the bit after Christmas, that bit in between
where humanity's a mixture of confusion and cheese.
What's the time? What's the day? What year are we in?
Shall we all have a cuppa? Maybe make mine a gin.

I am woman hear me ~~ROAR~~

I am woman hear me ~~roar~~
diminish myself,
berate myself,
not trust my intuition,
worry I'm too much,
worry I'm not enough,
question my agenda,
compare myself to others,
underestimate myself,
second-guess myself,
seek permission,
hold myself to impossible standards;
hear me live and play out the script that society heaps on me
to keep me small and submissive
because if I ever realise my true
God-given,
Heaven-kissed,
Spirit-breathed potential,
it will change the world.

Your rest will lead to your restoration.

Heavy

If you feel heavy,
perhaps it is from
the weight of carrying
unrealistic and unkind
expectations of yourself.

Life Admin

My head is full of lots of things
and round and round they spin,
they take up space and pick up pace,
they call it life admin.

Like making sure we have clean pants
and that the chicken has defrosted,
pairing of socks, batteries for clocks
ensure all birthday cards are posted.

I know that we could get
our wifi cheaper somewhere else instead,
that's just one more thing,
of life admin,
that lives inside my head.
The online shop, the mouldy mop,
the Calpol needs replacing,
buy rabbit food and sink un-blocker,
wipe the toothpaste off the basin.
The eldest has outgrown his jeans,
the youngest needs new trainers,
the lego has gotten everywhere,
I must buy new containers.

So if you see I'm tired and snappy,
that simply is a code
to communicate
I'm just worn out
from this heavy mental load.

Home

I will not contort and twist,
in order to fit the places and spaces
that I have outgrown.
I will honour the fingerprints of my maker,
as I make the journey home
to my truest self.
It will be my act of worship.

The world needs you to show up,

just as you are.

Mothers Day

Mums, they come in different sizes,
many forms and diverse guises,
mums who juggle and feel close to breaking,
mums with empty arms whose hearts are aching,
and some who every month are still waiting-
waiting.

Mums who rubbed their growing bumps
who pee a little when they jump,
mums who grew children in their hearts,
some who have their reasons to live apart,
those who open up their arms and homes,
to ensure no child ever feels alone,
those who have felt the sting of pain,
and who long to hold their child again.

So many ways to be a mother
all beautiful, all powerful, all different from each other.

On Weight and Worth

I've lost count of my daily steps
on scales cold and unwelcoming,
ready to find my worth in abstract numbers that silently stare back at me,
congratulating me on shrinking or berating me for taking up space.
So today as I hovered my foot,
ready to find my worth in my gravitational pull,
I refused and resisted.
And placed my foot back on that solid ground,
on words full of grace and truth
that lift my face and remind me
that if I look for my worth there,
I will forever be searching.

Liberation

It is liberating to realise
that you do not need anyone's permission
to grow,
to change,
to evolve,
to choose.
You are free to live
widely,
expansively,
authentically-
fully.

**Your holy growth
may be wholly inconvenient
for others.
Grow anyway.**

Overthinking

Sometimes, I tend to overthink
and make up stories in my head.
I assume the worst
and fill in the gaps
of all the things that were not said.
I second guess and analyse,
play guessing games and catastrophise,
and I know that this is just not wise,
though I am sure that I could earn first prize,
or at least a medal of some sort
if overthinking were a sport.

Skin

Oh I hope that today and everyday thereafter,
you feel at home
in your own skin,
knowing that you bear
the fingerprints
of the creator,
and that every inch of you
is glorious.

Grace

And yet, grace.
Regardless of what your day has looked like,
there is grace;
grace for the wandering and the wondering,
grace for the mark we missed,
grace for the standard we fell short of,
grace upon grace;
grace over the raised voice,
the clenched jaw and the harsh words;
grace to the ungracious and the undeserving,
unmerited favour to you even in your self-loathing;
grace for those that mourn and those that rejoice,
grace in the hurting, the healing and the waiting,
grace for the different seasons and stages,
for the failures and the successes.
He is good, He is kind and He longs to be gracious to you.

Self-advocacy is a powerful gesture.

She

She is fire and water. She is earth and gentle breeze.
She was crafted that way
by the one who calls her beloved
and whose fingerprints she bares
from her head to her feet.

Her feet are firmly planted on the earth,
yet still she has the knowledge
of what it is
to walk upon heavenly places,
so attuned is her heart to the things of Heaven.

With her heart soft and her mind spacious,
she is open and wild and her creativity flows.
She allows her maker to lead her in the ancient ways
and to remind her
that neither she nor he
belongs in a box, a building, or a book alone.

She is fire and water, she is earth and gentle breeze.
She is us.

Breathe

Today, I will breathe in my breath,
knowing that this act alone reflects that I am loved.
I will exhale the stories I tell myself that are as fickle and false as fake news.
I will exhale the second guessing and the watching myself being watched.
I will remember who I am and to whom I belong,
and in that truth I will live and breath and have my being.

Ever Curious

Today, may we be moved from resolute dogma to humble wonder,
released from the need to always be right,
from hard-hearted grand statements
that leave no room for the curious and the seeking.
Lead us away from the prison of cynicism,
and break us open into the wide open space of curiosity.
Make us at home in the mystery
and the glorious enormity of it all.
O God, keep us curious and ever curious.

**May the
YES
within you
declare itself.**

Fully

You need not
live your life
as a mere representative
when you are called
to show up
fully as yourself.

**May you know deep in your bones,
who you are,
and to whom you belong.**

Three

There at the beginning of all things,
brooding-
creating-
birthing-
divinely connected, divinely distinct: three.
I listen to her wind words,
her breath on my face
emboldening me, resuscitating what longs for fresh life.
She breathes the breath that ignites a thousand fires in me,
untangling me from all that so easily entangles;
comforting, convicting and leading me into truth.

Today,
would you be
a prisoner
to nothing
and to no one but
hope.

Eye to Eye

Lead me not into convenient individualism
and deliver me from entitlement.
Remind me to follow the way of self sacrifice,
of grace, mercy and of loving my neighbour,
even when we don't see eye to eye.

I will make my holy departure from people-pleasing, performative faith; and will instead walk into the wide open space of His transformative love.

An Ode to an iPhone

I don't want to be distracted
or to distance myself away from Your presence,
but I so often find myself
scrolling, searching, swiping,
adding to cart and refreshing,
Evenings of channel-hopping and Whatsapp-swapping
and yet another day goes by
with not much exchange between you and I.
I don't want that to be our story,
One of disconnect and untold glory,
I want to be captivated and connected,
my heart attuned to yours,
But it seems that history repeats itself,
As an apple gets in the way.

PRAYER & LITURGY

O God of all creation and all beginnings,
would You take my chaos
and create something beautiful.
Would You hover and brood over me,
as You did in the very beginning of time.
Will You create divine order
out of my human mess.
Would You speak light and life,
and growth and flourishing.
Would You breathe Your breath,
and may it sustain me all the days of my life.

Breathe in

Lord, You don't want more *from* me.

Breathe out

You desire more *for* me.

I give my hands to You,
with palms facing Heaven,
open to receiving what You have to give,
open to letting go
of what no longer serves me nor glorifies You.
Release from my grip
the people I am holding to ransom,
and the false expectations
that cause me disappointment and pain.
Remind me that there is always an invitation,
to let go,
to receive,
to lift my hands to Heaven.

THE CAMOUFLAGED SACRED

God who weeps,
disturb me from my privileged slumber,
and invite me to the holy practice
of weeping and mourning with those who do the same.
Help me to turn the other cheek but never a blind eye,
to the painful realities of the world,
both brutal and beautiful as it spins on its axis.
When my full belly weighs heavier than my heart,
when the privilege of my postcode passes me by,
would You interrupt me,
to remind me that the whole of the world is brother and sister,
all crafted and formed from the same star dust,
all containing-
Your sustaining breath.

God who deserves all our praise,
Help me to live a 'Hallelujah Anyway' type of life,
not out of agenda,
nor obligation,
but from the knowledge
of who You are
and Your vast, deep, wide, high, long love for me.

THE CAMOUFLAGED SACRED

Sometimes, God, I forget.
I forget to recount Your great faithfulness
and the times You have
rescued, restored and renewed me;
and so I find myself
in some kind of forgetfulness and fear.
I feel like I'm going it alone,
and almost like I can't ask You for what I truly need.
Would You deliver me from spiritual amnesia
and lead me to remembrance
of Your very present help
in all my times of need.

THE CAMOUFLAGED SACRED

O God,
would You help me
not to hide from myself,
not in my prayers,
nor in my internal or external conversations.
Give me courage
to face who I am,
and more courage again,
to yield to whom I am becoming.
Help me to accept my belovedness,
even amongst my mixed motives
and my failings and fragilities.
Help me to be with You,
and to allow You to be with me-
exactly as I am.

THE CAMOUFLAGED SACRED

Now is the occasion,
not tomorrow, or the next day,
nor one hundred days from now.
O God of all our days,
would You help me to see
and to celebrate
that this very present moment
is the occasion.
Give me the courage to show up
for the miracle of right now.

God of new mornings
and new mercies,
would You work within me today.
Soften my harsh edges.
Smooth out the rough.
Help me to lay down my weapon words,
my offences,
my defences,
in order that my heart,
and my hands are freed up,
so I can truly love.

THE CAMOUFLAGED SACRED

Save us from trinket gods
and magic show, fast food, let me entertain you religion.
Deliver us from being distracted by shiny novelties
and from the need to proclaim fullness
whilst our spiritual stomach rumbles.
May You place Your hands
on either side of my face,
and gently guide my gaze away
from anything that distracts and detracts
from knowing You fully.

Help me to position myself
under the abundant flow
of Your goodness and grace.
Help me not to disqualify myself,
thinking that I know more of me than You do.
You know it all
and still You draw me to Yourself.
I want to enter in.
I want to know the abundance of You.
Yet I find myself perpetually on the periphery,
on the outside looking in.
And it is there that I find it hard to keep my heart soft.
It is there that I find cynicism begins to take hold
and in all of my humanness I feel an outsider of Your love.
So help me.
Do not grow weary with me and my harsh edges.
Invite me again and again and yet again.

THE CAMOUFLAGED SACRED

O God,
who is the narrator of all sacred mysteries,
help me to take my place
in the beautiful story You are crafting.
I empty myself
of all the false and fake stories
that I have the tendency to write myself.
Give me eyes to see,
and ears to really hear
the truth of the story older than time itself.
Give me courage to step into the narrative.
Give me wisdom to play my part.

Breathe in

When I am exhausted

Breathe out

Lord, be my strength.

THE CAMOUFLAGED SACRED

Oh God whose love is vast and wide and deep and long,
who chose to identify with Your creation,
to hunger, to weep,
to feel the very weight of the human condition.
God, who both ate at tables
and turned the tables of the ones who oppressed the ones You ate with.
You were incarnated to free the incarcerated,
You see through titles and rituals and straight to the sin in the system.
You set captives free.
You bind up the broken-hearted.
You are still working to see justice roll like a river.

Remind me, God,
that You are a safe place.
I need Your shelter.
Remind me, God,
that I am loveable.
I need Your grace.
Remind me, God,
that all will be well.
I need Your reassurance.
Remind me, God,
that I am not too far away for You to reach me.
I need Your tender touch.
Remind me
that You are slow to anger and abounding in love.
I need a true perspective of You.
Remind me of who You are.
I need reminding.

God we thank you for 67 million beating hearts in this nation;
for 67 million precious people who bear Your fingerprints and have gifts to be discovered, stories to be redeemed and an eternity ahead of them.
We think of our neighbours, our family, our colleagues, especially the one that is hard to get on with.

We think of those incarcerated either in their circumstances or in prisons: those that feel trapped and are looking for a way out.
We pray especially for those who are planning their way out of life. Lord, would You be as close as their breath.
We think of Your precious people in hospitals asking big questions of their lives and their deaths.

We think of those who feel falsely fulfilled with what the world offers them and for those who feel utterly empty.
We think of the the youngest to the oldest,
for the one breathing their first breath and the one breathing their last.
And as Your eyes roam to and fro across the earth not missing a single beat, we ask, Lord, that You would remind each and every one of us of Your lavish, no-holds-barred love for us all.
Show up in our dreams, our conversations, our memories of songs sung in old school assemblies.
Thank You for how You are going to move and how You have moved in the past.
Thank You for thin places and holy spaces
where a sense of Your presence has brought people to their knees.

Show up here, there and everywhere and give our nation eyes to see You.
We repent of any rhetoric that has declared You are not welcome in our nation, in our schools, in our governance and systems and structures.
Reveal to us as a nation that things only make sense with You in the mix.

We pray for more of the unexpected,
for the local supermarket to host Your presence and for people to encounter You as they buy their milk and bread.
We pray for hearts to be strangely warmed.
We even dare to believe for some Damascus road experiences.
Inconvenience us with a hunger that can't be satisfied by fast food religion or trinket gods, Netflix or golden calves or golden anything.
We pray that You would draw people to You in weird and wonderful ways-
we love the way You work.

God who is gracious and kind,
I desire to reflect You today.
Would You remind me
at every twist and turn,
that I am crafted and created in Your image.
May I live out of the knowledge that I am enormously loved, wholly accepted and covered in outrageous grace.

Lord grant me the type of resilience that comes
not from gritting my teeth but from relaxing my jaw.
The righteous resilience of letting go and breathing deep,
safe in the knowledge that as I breath in my breath,
You are working all things for good
for I love you so.

Release my hands from their white knuckle grip.
I relinquish my own attempts at resilience
for it has left me bruised and tired.
My fingers hurt from holding on.
May I not prefer my grit
over Your grace.

May my resilience not look like the worldliness
of bounce back ability nor
the wilderness of the hustle and scrape.
May it instead look more like leaning and cleaving to You,
the resting of my head in your lap.

Remove from me I pray,
with gentle scalpel and tender touch,
the reflex to reach for my own resilience,
and the striving for strength all of my own.
Soften the harsh edges
that I have wilfully called resilience.
I welcome the holy work of Your hands.
And when I'm tempted to outwork
my attempts at resilience
in the 'get up and go',
in the 'keep calm and carry on'

or the 'just do it',
help me to remember
that I need not dig deep in me
for what can only be found in You.

When I feel just a little bit lost
and like I can't quite find myself,
may You come and find me. Seek me out.
Would Your words of grace and truth
wash over me and bring to my remembrance
who You say I am.

When I feel overwhelmed
to the point of simmering resentment,
when the demands of the day
make me feel like I don't even belong to myself,
would You place Your hands
on either side of my face and redirect my gaze.
Remind me that I am Yours and You call me beloved.

When I get caught in swiping and scrolling,
in comparing and contrasting
until the sense of my own discontent grows,
O God, would You meet me in that place
and whisper to me that I have all that I need.
The boundary lines have indeed fallen
in pleasant places for me.
Remind me of my delightful inheritance,
for You call me daughter.

When I feel like I have missed the mark,
when my disappointment takes hold,
when I wonder if I'm invisible
and I long to be seen,
may I know that You are El Roi:
the God who sees.

Will You meet me in my disappointment,
and may You delight in reappointing me
to my rightful place
of knowing exactly who I am
and to whom I belong.

God of all creation,
maker of me and of Heaven and Earth,
we fix our eyes on You.
We slow down our rhythm
to get in step with Your Spirit

You alone are God. I put my trust in You.

Make Your presence known.
In this sacred space of sitting still,
remind me to unclench my jaw,
to relax my shoulders
and to posture myself under Your sovereignty and kindness.
Help me to remember
in my body, soul and spirit,
the eternal invitation
to be still and know that You are God.

You alone are God. I put my trust in You.

Loving God,
we remember that You are living water that refreshes us,
holy fire that refines us.
You are the still, small voice that whispers in the wind,
the maker of Heaven and Earth on which I place my feet.
Creator of life, we breathe in Your goodness
and place our life flow in Your hands today.

You alone are God. I put my trust in You.

Let our lives collide with You at every turn.

Let my soul glorify You.
Let my spirit rejoice in You.
Let my body find rest in You,
in my sitting and my rising,
in my waking and my sleeping.

You alone are God. I put my trust in You.

O giver of breath, we praise You.
We stand in awe of Your 'yes' to us.
Very word that became flesh,
that knew both womb and world,
we marvel at Your gift of life.
We are humbled at Your invitation
to procreation and co-creation.
May the truth of Your generosity lead us to our knees, God.

O giver of breath, we praise You.

As we nurture this child, may we also know Your nurturing touch.
As we marvel at tiny fingers and delicate toes,
let us remember that we too, are fearfully and wonderfully made.
As we sing and we soothe
at dusk and into the dawn,
remind us that You are the God who does not slumber,
that You sing an eternal melody over us also.

O giver of breath, we praise You.

You knit this child together in the secret place.
You tenderly whispered life, hope, future:
days that are destined,
intrinsic gifts to unwrap.
Grant us grace
to hear the echoes of these whispers
as we seek to raise this child
into the fullness of all You intended.

Would each extension of our love
usher in Your kingdom,
Your power,
Your glory.
Great is Your faithfulness.
Abounding is Your love.

O giver of breath, we praise You.

Maker of Heaven & Earth,
keep us curious.
Not only observers in all You have created,
but instead active participants and pilgrims,
eyes and heart attuned.
O God, keep us curious and ever curious.

Move us from resolute dogma to humble wonder.
Release us from the need to be right,
from hard-hearted grand statements
that leave no room for the curious and the seeking.
Lead us away from the prison of cynicism
and break us open into the wide open space of curiosity.
Make us at home in the mystery
and the glorious enormity of it all.
O God, keep us curious and ever curious.

Keep us from the soporific slumber
of assumption and presumption;
instead, engaging in the holy work
of being fully awake,
of rolling up our sleeves
and asking the big questions.
Grant us that we may be
receptive and soft-hearted enough
to see that big answers
can appear in the seemingly small,
that miracles reside in the mundane,
the sacred sometimes camouflaged.
O God, keep us curious and ever curious.

May our curiosity lead us to love more expansively,
to live more wholeheartedly.
May it lead us to a place
where there is always room to be surprised
in a way that leads us to our knees.

Today, make us curious and ever curious.

**Sometimes, the truest prayer from the deepest part of myself is:
Lord, do You love me?**

With this new day may I know
new mercies, new hopes
and new possibilities ahead.

With the dawning of a fresh week, may I know
fresh creativity, fresh insights,
and a fresh sense of holy adventure.

With all the possibilities contained
in a day yet to unfold,
may I know the courage
to fully embrace the gift of life
in both its beauty and brutality.
May I keep my heart soft amidst the tension of the two
as I bring my unique contribution to this day
and to every day thereafter.

"When life is heavy and hard to take, go off by yourself. Enter the silence. Bow in prayer. Don't ask questions: Wait for hope to appear. Don't run from trouble. Take it full-face. The "worst" is never the worst."
Lamentations 3:28-30 MSG

Very present God,
closer than my own breath,
help me to enter in,
lead me to sit,
to bow low,
to quiet myself,
to un-busy my soul and un-bury my head.
Grant me the grace to lament the truth of my pain
held in the knowledge that it will not devour me.
You have no need for me to censor myself.
Remind me, O God, that the waiting room for hope is a holy place and You are here:
present, tender, kind.
I lift my heart and my hands.
Your stockpiles of loyal love are my sustenance.
You are my portion.
I will lean in.
I will wait for you.
For you usher in hope, new mornings and new mercies.
You, O God, will have the final say.

Breathe in

Even in my worst moments,

Breathe out

I am still completely loved.

THE CAMOUFLAGED SACRED

O creator of all life and creator of me,
we come to You today and ask You to remind us of the
fingerprints that we bear,
from our heads to our feet,
on our bodies, our spirits and our souls.

We don't always know how to hold the tension,
the tension of knowing that it was You who formed us
and yet, the deep feeling of being both not enough or perhaps
too much.
We so easily forget that we are holy nations, co-creators and
royal priesthoods.
And so we scroll, and we hustle.
We shrink back or puff up.
We hide and we hold ourselves up to the artificial light of
outward appearances
instead of the light of Your truth and Your grace.

We get tripped up by scarcity and begin to withhold in the fear
that there is not enough.
We limp away from the table still clutching our contributions.
Something fades away;
the light dims,
and the temptation to compare overarches and overwhelms.
We remain still and small
on the days where we feel the weight of expectations
against the knowledge of our limitations.
May we know Your grace
in the times where the voice of all we are not
feels deafening against the catchy song of all that we 'should'
be,

and the lure of all we 'could' be.
May we be still and know
the truth that is written in our very DNA:
I am Yours,
You are mine.
My place is found in the narrative of eternity.

May the unfolding revelation of who and whose I am
lead me to a spacious and open place.
May I be so beautifully captivated with purpose
that comparison has no choice but to expose itself as a thief and
a liar.
O God who delights in me and calls me by name,
enable me to pause and catch just a glimpse of that delight
in order for me to fully embody myself
as the temptation to compare- fades away.

For you created my inmost being;
you knit me together in my mother's womb.
I praise you because I am fearfully and wonderfully made;
your works are wonderful

*I know that full well.
My frame was not hidden from you
when I was made in the secret place,
when I was woven together in the depths of the earth.
Your eyes saw my unformed body;
 all the days ordained for me were written in your book
before one of them came to be.
How precious to me are your thoughts, God!
How vast is the sum of them!
Were I to count them,
they would outnumber the grains of sand—
When I awake, I am still with you.
Psalm 139*

And as we accept ourselves, may it
pour out through our interactions with others.
May the compassion towards our glorious imperfections
manifest into compassion towards others.
For it is in my weakness that you are strong
and, in a wonderfully upside-down Kingdom way,
it is through my imperfections that you are glorified.

**May my life bear witness
to your goodness
and your grace.**

Breathe in

Oh that my life would be,

Breathe out

a living monument to your faithfulness.

Acknowledgements

I love the message paraphrase of Psalm 100, "Enter with the password 'Thank You'," and although slightly out of context here it does show us the importance and the power of thanks and gratitude.

I have also come to quite like the long genealogies in scripture, every name mentioned is a precious beating heart, an individual, an image-bearer of God.

Thank you's matter.
Names matter.

So firstly, the name above all names: Father, Son and Holy Spirit, I give thanks upon thanks, upon thanks.

My husband Dan and my sons and daughter, thank you for letting me hide in the downstairs loo to write. Thank you for being gracious with all of my *just one more minute*s, but mostly, thank you for all that you are and all that you will be. You are my biggest inspiration.

Thank you to my Year 3 teacher who accused me of copying my first poem. There is nothing like a little bit of adversity and injustice to get me motivated.

Thank you to my side-running sister Leah Boden for her encouragement and for writing the most wonderful foreword. And to Stuart, Matt, Clare, Connie, Sally and Meghan for their most encouraging and kind endorsements, thank you.

Thank you to Duane White who prophetically called out this book before I had even put pen to paper, thank you for seeing what I didn't see.

Lastly, and of course nowhere-near-leastly, a huge, outrageous, indebted, deeply grateful thank you to Joseph and Meghan Bell, who have been a creative force, an encouraging voice, a wise counsel, and wonderful friends from start to finish. Thank you for late night editing, for pouring over rewrites and tedious grammatical errors, for designing and redesigning and for being so gracious and patient in the process.

About the Author

Joanna Hargreaves is a writer, a pastor and a therapist. Her work, already widely shared on social media, expresses the often unspoken elements of life and faith. With characteristic authenticity and relatability, she weaves together the sacred and mundane, shining a light on the way God moves in our everyday.

Joanna's prayer is that this book finds you exactly where you are.

Joanna would love to connect with you and hear your stories.

You can find her here:

Instagram: @johargreaves

Email: camouflagedsacred@gmail.com

Facebook: https://www.facebook.com/joanna.hargreaves.52

Please feel free to share her writing on social media ensuring you link, tag and credit her work as well as using the hashtag:

#TheCamouflagedSacred

Printed in Great Britain
by Amazon